Healing & Mystical States
Are Just a Breath Away:
Personal Experiences with
Holotropic Breathwork™

Andy Grant

"The human psyche shows that each individual is an extension of all of existence."
~ Stanislav Grof

Disclaimer and Terms of Use:

The Author and Publisher has strived to be as accurate and complete as possible in the creation of this book. While all attempts have been made to verify information provided in this publication, the Author and Publisher assume no responsibility for errors, omissions, or contrary interpretation of the subject matter herein. Any perceived slights of specific persons, peoples, or organizations are unintentional.

In practical advice books, like anything else in life, there are no guarantees of results. Readers are cautioned to rely on their own judgment about their individual circumstances and act accordingly.

This book is for informational purposes only and is not intended for use as a source of legal, business, medical or financial advice. All readers are advised to seek services of competent professionals in legal, business, medical and finance fields.

"Holotropic Breathwork" is a trademark of Stanislav Grof and Christina Grof.

Printed in the United States of America

Paperback Edition, April 2014

Table of Contents

Preface

    I had never heard of Holotropic Breathwork™ before I did it my first time, but it was nothing short of life changing. I didn't even seek out more information or read about Holotropic Breathwork until after doing it my second time. As of this writing I've done it seven times, have gotten my wife to take part in it, have made fantastic lasting friendships with people I've breathed with and tell everyone I know to try it themselves.

    If you aren't familiar with Holotropic Breathwork, it is a group process of deep accelerated breathing and loud evocative music that puts breathers into non-ordinary states of consciousness where amazing things can happen. I find it to be the most transformative and healing experience I've ever come across. It allows for an inner journey, which often seems like a psychedelic trip, yet involves no drugs or alcohol. Solely your own breath fuels your adventure.

    Because my experiences have been so amazing, healing and beneficial I decided to share my personal experience in an effort to get more people to have their own encounter with Holotropic Breathwork.

These are my experiences, often left exactly as I wrote them in my journal moments after my breathing sessions. Some passages are blog posts I wrote a day or two after breathing. Your breathing sessions and experiences will be different. But you'll never know unless you try.

One bit of warning – there are many different breathwork workshops, seminars, and books, I am referring only to certified Holotropic Breathwork. The certification process to be a facilitator is years long. Do not just read a book on Holotropic Breathwork and attempt to do it on your own or with some friends. Do this in a safe environment with well-trained professionals.

This second edition adds an additional chapter as I've experienced Holotropic Breathwork once more since originally writing this.

Breath on,

Andy Grant

April, 2014

"The difference between a mystic and a lunatic is that the mystic knows who to tell."

~ Stanislav Grof

CHAPTER ONE

What is Holotropic Breathwork?

To me, Holotropic Breathwork is the most incredible, mystical experience I've encountered in my life. It is a psychedelic trip without the use of any drugs. It is the most relaxing meditative state I've ever been in. Holotropic Breathwork is a rebirthing experience. It is a deep and profound emotional and spiritual healing of the self. Holotropic Breathwork has been all of these things for me, because each time I've taken part in the practice, I've had a unique experience.

Holotropic Breathwork is a practice that uses breathing and other elements to allow access to non-ordinary states of consciousness for the purpose of self-exploration, personal transformation and healing. It was developed by Stanislav Grof, M.D., Ph.D. and

Christina Grof, Ph.D., leading pioneers in the field of Transpersonal Psychology. Holotropic Breathwork integrates insights from modern consciousness research, anthropology, various depth psychologies, transpersonal psychology, Eastern spiritual practices, and mystical traditions. The term holotropic means, "moving toward wholeness" (from the Greek holos "whole" and trepein "to turn or direct towards a thing").

The process itself is quite simple: it combines accelerated breathing in a group setting with evocative music in a special set. With the eyes closed and lying on a mat, each person uses their own breath and the music in the room to enter a non-ordinary state of consciousness. This state activates the natural inner healing process of the individual's psyche, bringing him or her a particular set of internal experiences. With the inner healing intelligence guiding the process, the quality and content brought forth is unique to each person and for that particular time and place. While recurring themes are common, no two sessions are ever alike.

The method also includes focused bodywork, mandala drawing, and group sharing. The breathwork's general effect is advocated as an amplification of a person's psychic process, which facilitates the psyche's natural capacity for healing. We all have an inner healer that will allow only what we can handle to come to the surface to be experienced, released and healed.

Holotropic Breathwork is usually done in groups with people in the group working together in pairs alternating in the roles of "breather" and "sitter". The sitter's primary responsibility is to focus compassionate attention on the breather. Secondarily, the sitter is available to assist the breather, but not to interfere or interrupt the process. The same is true for trained facilitators, who are available as helpers if necessary. A session goes for 2 to 3 hours then participants swap roles for a session later that same day or the following day, depending on the specific workshop.

Originally developed as an adjunct to psychedelic psychotherapy, Holotropic Breathwork is an autonomous psychotherapeutic practice with many years of clinical practice behind it. I'll share a list of books, websites and more in the Resources section.

While it is simple and quite easy for most people to participate in, the years of training required for facilitators is extensive. I mentioned this in the forward, but it bears repeating; don't underestimate the powerful effects of breathwork and attempt to do this alone or with untrained people. With that warning out of the way, let's dive into the fun.

CHAPTER TWO

The First Time

The following are a series of journal entries and blog posts I wrote following my first Holotropic Breathwork experience which was done midway through a week-long meditation retreat with Centerpointe Research Institute in October of 2008. Centerpointe are the creators of the Holosync meditation CD's which I've been using daily since August, 2007.

THURSDAY, OCTOBER 23, 2008

Oh My God!

I've passed the half way mark of my Centerpointe Retreat week. We've done hours of Holosync each day, much more powerful levels than I have at home and each session has been totally unique. Sometimes I fall asleep and almost fall out of my chair, other times I'm running thoughts and song lyrics in my head the whole time and others I'm just in this wild, blank zone of emptiness. Tonight we did a different sort of meditation, one based on circular breathing for two hours. You breathe very full and deep and don't pause at any time, so air is constantly circulating through you and it can result in some altered states.

It sure worked for me. Tonight was the most amazing experience I've ever had in my life. It was a total out-of-body, flying around experience seeing all sorts of crazy shit and totally freaking out for a three-hour ride. It was so bizarre and awesome; thrilling and scary all at once. It was like jumping out of an airplane on mushrooms.

My original partner decided to opt of this exercise because she had done something similar to it previously and didn't like it much. I was teamed with a married couple of wily veterans, Patti and Allen, who are part of the staff. Patti sat while Allen and I breathed. One of the last things she said to me was that it could get pretty wild as people get vocal, some screaming and crying. She warned me that it could sound like an insane asylum. I lay on some blankets along with about 35 other people in an empty banquet hall. Everyone but Allen and I had a single person sitting beside them to remind us to breathe, keep us in our spot, hand us water, help us to the bathroom or whatever else might come up. The lights were very dim and the music very loud. They cranked up all sorts of cool tribal music with drums, chants, didgeridoos and such.

I started off just doing the breathing, never pausing—deep full breaths lying flat on my back, still on the floor on a blanket and my head on a pillow. I had work thoughts in my head; answering emails that I'd read in my room after dinner. That kind of pissed me off so I was writing emails in my head, explaining that this breathwork was going on and I was too blissed out to give a shit about work and I wasn't going to look at anymore email till Saturday.

I pretty quickly lost sense of my body—my hands tingled and went numb first, then my arms, back, legs, everything. I could only feel some small back muscles getting used because I was breathing so deeply.

You breathe filling your belly, and without pausing at the top or bottom of each breath so it is always circulating. Deep full breaths, called Circular Breathing or Holotropic Breathing.

So I'm feeling out of my body, just floating and blissful. Then I'm flying—soaring thru darkness. Just in awe—feeling beauty and bliss. Feeling like THIS is life! Energy. Source. Just an extremely pleasant experience–reminiscent of Holosyncing on my deck in LaFuma antigravity recliners.

A couple times I felt like I jumped because I forgot to breathe. It really seemed like I missed a breath or two and my body lurched to catch up. That is when I thought I definitely have this thing working. At dinner someone who had done this before said at some point you can feel like your partner is breathing for you— that didn't make much sense to me. Maybe they were describing this sort of lost breath thing that I felt.

As the tribal music played I saw the Samburu and Masai dancers from Kenya–the long and thin bouncing bodies, the bright colors, the smiling faces. Then the Yugua tribe in the Amazon; the grass skirts, the old chiefs and young kids, the blow darts and Larry The Lizard fun. Then the Rappanui on Easter Island–the songs, our guide (the Ray Ramano look-a-like), the dinner dance—then I was fantasizing scenes having wild dancers in front of the Moai. Feeling really blessed and amazed with all the places I've been and people I've met. Then I recalled Katmandu–the children chasing me through the streets after Larry. Then I saw the third eye—the Buddha eye above me in a sea of black looking down.

That is when I knew I had some serious shit going on. It was fun and heavenly. Now and then work thoughts would creep in and I'd be pissed—say 'no way' and "I don't Give a Shit about Cisco."

Then I'd just be floating, flying, remembering and having a great time. Decided I want to go to Nepal again. Amazed we were there before I was into the more spiritual aspects of the place. I remembered and saw a couple favorite photos—me in a Metallica t-shirt hugging a smiling Tibetan priest, and then the Holy Man who looked like Charles Manson. Remembered my beard being long and local kids pulling on it, touching it and other Holy Men pointing at me.

Very Cool.

I have to go back to Nepal and find this dude.

Then in a pause or quiet moment in the music, I heard a few people in the room crying. I had a huge wave of compassion and concern…I was sad, but not for myself. I had a single tear roll down my face and I felt sad for these crying souls. I wanted to know what was wrong. I wanted to go give them a hug and make them feel better. I wanted everyone to experience the absolute Joy I was feeling. Patti put one hand on my chest and wiped the tears away with the other.

Then I heard a real creepy, crazy wail. I remembered Patti warning me earlier that people will make noises and it could sound like an insane asylum.

I thought—wow, that pained howl DOES sound like an asylum. Then I got huge wave of despair, guilt, and horror that I KNEW what an insane asylum sounded like.

From that point on, I alternate between joy/bliss and tears/pain. For the joy—I felt how AMAZING life is. I felt so AWESOME, Pure Bliss. And I thought, "I can't believe I tried to throw this away." That's when the bottom fell out. I could barely breathe—fought sobs and tears. I could feel two people at times touching me, rubbing my head and Patti even sang in my ear at one point—unless I imagined it.

This was like a dream with narration and awareness. I could think anything I wanted; I knew where I was and what I was doing. I would quicken my breath or breath even deeper to make shit happen or try to see if it made a difference in my experience. Those were tips from Patti before we started, she said my own breathing would drive the ship and I could slow or speed up the whole experience.

For what seemed like hours, I bounced between bliss and sadness. I just had to think, "I tried to throw this away," and I'd cry again. Then moments later I'd be smiling. I thought of asking Michael (an intuitive songwriter at the retreat) for another song—about the guilt of hurting people who love you, over trying to hurt yourself—more tears. But I kept stopping my tears from really flowing and crying. Lying flat on my back I couldn't really sob and breathe. Tears would stream for a few seconds, then I got control—buried something back up. But I kept intentionally going back to that thought to test and push myself. "I can't believe I tried to throw this away."

For what seemed like the first time in my life, I saw that life was BEAUTIFUL. A gift. Perfection. And it absolutely broke my heart that I had tried to end it. I was soaring through life. It was like I could smell colors and see emotions.

I imagined trying to write about the experience I was having and it made me cry. I knew any description would never do it justice. I imagined thanking Patti at the end—and I cried. I imagined people asking about this next week and me just crying thinking about it.

All the adventures, thrills, drugs, scares...I've ever done pale in comparison to what I was going through.

I was expansive, limitless, timeless...

I thought of the movie "Contact" when Jodi Foster comes into contact with an alien presence or world and says "They should have sent a poet" with a single tear on her face. I didn't get that line when I first saw it. Now I'm living it. Wow.

There was one point when the music stopped and I thought—it must be over, but I'm not leaving this. I'll make someone tell me it's over, I'm not going to open my eyes and ruin this most amazing feeling. Then the music started up again. I later learned that was indeed the scheduled 10pm end time but a few people were still going so they played some more music.

Finally, the music stopped for good and I felt Patti rubbing my right shoulder. It was both hands and a little more forceful than the gentle touches I'd been receiving. I knew she was trying to rouse me back to "the world." But I still didn't want it to end. I wanted to stay here in the bliss land. I wanted to stay for as long as I could. Forever.

When I did open my eyes—I felt SO out of it. Just beyond words—totally loopy, blurry vision, the room was still dim and it was like my eyes had star filters on them. First I just saw the ceiling and had no idea what it was. Then I saw Doris's face on my left, (she's the psychologist running the session) and was sure I was still sleeping/dreaming/ whatever...I thought she was an angel. It was only when I saw Patti to my right that I was sure my eyes were open and that this was real.

Patti smiled and said, "You got your money's worth"

I turned my head to look around and saw that all the other participants were gone. I opened my mouth to say... something and just started crying. Heavy sobbing. I tried to sit up and my back screamed in pain. Doris said "slow, easy, keep breathing" Then as if on cue I stopped breathing—panic and sobs hit all at once—it was very bizarre. I was sobbing in such a freakish no-breath way. I couldn't make myself breathe. For a second I felt panic that I broke something, that I had somehow forgotten how to breathe normally and I was just going to suffocate. Sort of thought, "oh wow, after everything I'm just going to die right here and now." It was a strangely calm thought, just "Oh well."

After what felt like minutes, but I'm sure was a split second, I was able to breathe again. I moved my head slowly from side to side, wiggled my fingers and toes, picked up my hands and moved my legs a bit. Then would cry some more. I tried to sit up and just couldn't...a combination of pain and not knowing what to do...I finally spit out, "I've forgotten how to sit up."

I had to roll over onto my side, and then move to my hands and knees. Patti handed me some water. I tried to say thanks, I think, and cried some more. My hands shook as I drank. I got to my feet, then quickly got back down to my knees and laughed. Gravity felt wrong. I gave it another try and made it up for good, but I was very wobbly and uncoordinated. I was alternating between laughing at it all and still having tears stream down my face. I took a few steps and thought I was going to fall–it was just so wild! I couldn't believe I was the last person in the room. I felt like I was having a drug and booze binge hangover, while being sedated and walking on the moon.

Doris and Patti helped me gather my belongings together. Patti helped me walk towards my room, but we stopped and sat on a couch for a few minutes. I sobbed heavily for another burst or a second or two. She said that's what I'd been doing for a couple of hours–short bursts of sobs. She told me to expect more of that and to not try to stop it. She verified that I didn't move at all during the breathwork and that I had been smiling at times.

After a few minutes I decided I was good enough to go to my room, I wanted to write as much down as I could before I forgot it all.

A 3 hour tour. The most outrageous and beautiful experience I've ever had.

AMAZING.

I kept crying off and on thru the night. Wanting to capture every bit that I could, I wrote in my journal deep into the early morning. I wrote letters to my mother and father, telling them how sorry I was for what I'd done and asking for forgiveness. I sent them each a dozen roses. For the first time in my life, I mourned my suicide attempts. I felt the pain of being both inside of and outside of me during those periods.

I could tell something huge had shifted. I gave myself credit for surviving attempted murder.

The next morning we were asked to put our experience to paper, in a circle drawing called a mandala. Here is mine.

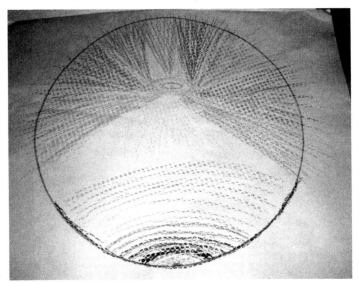

My first mandala

BLOG POST - SATURDAY, OCTOBER 25, 2008

An Amazing End to an Amazing Week

Good God what a day! Today alone felt like it was a week long. The Centerpointe Retreat officially ended tonight with a celebration and impromptu talent show (that I actually participated in!). Considering that at 11am this morning I was standing on that very stage sobbing uncontrollably in front of 60+ people and then managed to hopefully entertain them from the same spot tonight with some of my Hollywood tales and bad acting displays is almost beyond my comprehension. This is the final retreat Centerpointe is doing, so it was extra emotional for all the staff too. I feel so grateful for having been here.

I tried to come into this week with no expectations; with one goal—to force myself to fully participate and go beyond my comfort zone. Believe me there were plenty of times I just wanted to run away; even one time that I actually did. Some of the exercises we did just flat out sucked, but the fantastic group of people here made them suck less. I'm leaving with so much more than I ever dreamed. Along with just an astounding, mystical experience Wednesday night, I've got a second mom down in Kentucky, and many new powerful life-long connections with people I didn't even know a week ago. There is one person I can't even look at without breaking into tears because she is so amazing, and I've known her for all of 48 hours. I'm even friends with a Lakers fan (ugh!). Most of the day I was on a hair trigger, crying without warning at any moment. By dinner people were telling me I was glowing. Bill Harris even called me Buddha.

I'll see most people again at breakfast, which is just a few hours away at this point, and then it's back home to Boston via Washington DC. I'm supposed to go to the Patriots game Sunday, but I can't see caring about that at all. As I said, in tears of course, at the goodbye ceremony tonight, "I feel sorry for the poor schmuck sitting next to me on the flight home."

BLOG POST - SUNDAY, OCTOBER 26, 2008

Awareness or Acid?

Well, I'm back home safe and sound. I've been up since before 5am which was quite a surprise since I'd only slept 3 hours the night before. Still don't feel quite "right" or "normal", but maybe this is the new "normal". It's like I'm on some low level acid trip— everything is noticeably brighter, sharper, deeper. Flying yesterday was fantastic and thrilling. It was like it was my first flight ever; at times I was staring out the window gawking at the clouds and sky in amazement with a big shit-eating grin on my face. And music, God, music is just so much more moving— every lyric is stunning. The only poor schmuck sitting with me who had to put up with my smiling, singing and tears was me. Luckily I had a row to myself on the first flight. Second flight was a different story, but I didn't care by then. I was in my own space and enjoying the madness. Not sure if people didn't notice me or were too scared to look my way.

When I landed at Logan, nothing seemed familiar. It was like I landed in some new city. Lori picked me up for the drive home. I didn't even try to speak to her until a few minutes passed and even then could only spit out a couple words. I was mesmerized by the lights, it seemed like Boston had turned into Las Vegas while I was away. There were amazing bright neons everywhere that I had never noticed before. It was as if I'd flash forwarded fifty years and was seeing some blazingly vibrant city of the future. As we got closer to home the wind really picked up and all the leaves being blown across the road were dazzling. I'd swear some of them were alive; little critters scurrying across the road—I was pretty close to freaking out at this point. But they were so neat to look at, it wasn't anything frightening.

I'm now thinking this is raised awareness—feelings that were always here but buried. Now I really get why so many people do drugs—it's to feel this. But it's always been here, waiting to be found. Not everyone had such an experience from the circular breathing; some people simply had a relaxing time, others had frightening visions of demons, rape, and death, some had very physical reactions even lashing out in violence. So this isn't to be taken lightly and I'm very grateful for my experience. I can't imagine having some horrifying vision last week only to return home to neighborhoods decorated for Halloween. I look forward to trying it all again, soon.

BLOG POST - TUESDAY, OCTOBER 28, 2008

Coming in for a Landing

Well, the flying goat I've been riding seems to be finally coming in for a landing. Today is the most normal I've felt since sometime last Wednesday. The last big hallucinations were Sunday afternoon; all the leaves on the trees around my house were waving at me. Scratch that; it was actually only the yellow and gold leaves that were waving. Guess the red, orange and brown leaves aren't my biggest fans.

For a while I was totally mesmerized by the feeling of my pants against my legs—I was aware of each hair and skin cell as the fabric moved against them. I was as close to just completely freaking out as I could be about that time. Even last night I could see beams of light from all the light bulbs in my house. I'd burst out laughing and Lori would ask what was so funny, but I could never explain it.

Apart from that sort of hyper-awareness, everything is still rather amazing. Whatever I do or see feels like it's the first time. Yesterday my office phone rang (Thank God, I work from home or I'd have to take this whole week off probably) and I was just blown away. I didn't know what to do. I noticed colored lights on the phone that I'd swear weren't there before and I was dumbfounded as to what to do next. Granted this phone is a little different, I could answer with the handset or pick a set of headphones, but I had to think and notice it all before I could decide how to answer the phone. Almost everything has been like that. The first time I answered an email yesterday... I was thrilled! I was as proud as if I'd completed some major research paper or something. Just so...wild.

But it is settling down. This morning I was taking Homer for a walk. In the driveway it started raining and I thought about going back inside. Then I realized; I didn't feel wet. I could see and hear that it was raining rather hard, but not on me. So we walked on and of course it was amazing. At one point I thought someone was behind me, I turned and a single gold leaf was falling and twirling right past my face. It reminded me of the dancing plastic bag in "American Beauty". I thought that scene was so stupid with the kid in tears about how beautiful the trash was. Needless to say, I don't feel like that anymore. :)

I even 'synced again last night for the first time since Friday, later Lori shook me awake because my whole body was lurching, jumping to catch some missed breath like when I did the circular breathing at the retreat. Bizarro.

So beyond my occasional communication with leaves, every thing's back to normal.

Looking Back

It wasn't until over four years later that I realized what that amazing, blissful feeling I was soaring through in my breathwork was. It was love. I had tapped into the unending, unconditional love the universe has for us all. I was in love with all of life. I was in love with myself. That feeling was missing, completely cut off, in my suicidal times.

I returned home from that week burst open, so many things happened besides the Holotropic Breathwork, and since most people there called it circular breathing I forgot the real name and never looked for more information on it. I thought it was something that would never cross my path again.

CHAPTER THREE

The Second Time

In 2010, I got a catalog from Kripalu Center for Yoga and Health in western Massachusetts, which is about two hours away from my home. I'd heard of it on occasion but had never been there. A weekend of Holotropic Breathwork was coming with its creator, Dr. Stanislav Grof. I had never heard of him but was thrilled to have the opportunity to breathe again and was sure doing it with the person who developed it would make it extra cool.

Here is the description of the program:

This is a rare invitation to experience Holotropic Breathwork with Stanislav Grof. This practice, originated by Stanislav Grof and Christina Grof, allows direct access to your own inner healing wisdom. Through simple breathing, a specially designed

*musical journey, and a safe and supportive setting
with trained facilitators, you experience a true non-
ordinary state of consciousness, allowing deep self-
exploration, personal transformation, and healing.*

*The weekend begins with a talk by Stanislav on the
healing potential of non-ordinary states of
consciousness and preparation for the breathwork
that will take place on Saturday morning and
afternoon. Sunday morning features small-group
integration and large-group lecture and questions. In a
breathwork session, your wisdom brings you a unique
and ideal combination of experiences that can include
aspects of your personal history, psychological death
and rebirth, transpersonal interconnections, and the
greater spiritual reality to which we all belong.*

I had no idea what to expect from the sequel,
which is what made it so exciting. Thinking back to
what I went through the first time—my only concern
was if I'd be able to drive myself home come Sunday.

BLOG POST - SATURDAY, OCTOBER 02,
2010

The Holotropic Sequel

It has been a week since my Holotropic
Breathwork weekend at Kripalu and I'm finally ready
to describe the experience, or at least try to. This was

my second time doing breathwork and this round was as awe-inspiring as my first time, while also being completely different.

Part of what made the weekend so cool was being able to hear directly from Stanislav Grof, a pioneer in transpersonal psychology, non-ordinary states and their healing potential, psychedelics research and about a dozen other things. He has written many books that you can dig into to learn about his research and experiences.

As for my experience; it began as all Holotropic Breathwork does, with me lying flat on my back on the floor in a large room with more than 100 other breathers and sitters. We are paired up, so each breather has a sitter to watch over them, and then we switch in the afternoon. You simply breathe deeper and faster than normal, keeping oxygen circulating through you; never pausing. They blast all sorts of cool tribal, mystical music for three hours and you just stay open to whatever happens.

Things started slow for me. I heard screams and sobs around me and a few songs into the session I wondered if I would feel anything except a nice, calm meditative state. I was sort of floating about blissfully. Then I had the weird urge to move and shimmy. In my first Holotropic experience I hadn't budged at all, so this was new. I squirmed left and right on my back and realized I couldn't separate my legs. I was a tadpole. I had this sense of swimming toward life. It was pleasant and fun. After a few minutes I felt arms grow but they seemed more like blunt clubs only, I couldn't do much with them. Then these pulses of energy, as if I was riding huge waves, swept through me. It felt like my spine was traveling along a roller coaster track, while at the same time I was in the world's strongest massage chair. My flesh felt like it was vibrating and being pulled back, as if I was leaving the launch pad headed into outer space. On the mat, I'm twitching with leg kicks and surges of energy down my entire body. I started flinging my arms up over my head in an alternating pattern as if I was doing the backstroke. Next came this tremendous pressure all over me, something pushing in against me from all sides. It was strongest at my head. I was scared and I thought "I don't want to go through this alone." The pressure intensified, my head felt like it was about to burst into flames. The fear increased, and then I felt the presence of my wife, Lori. I wanted to reach out to her and hold her hand, but I couldn't move. I wanted a hug. That is when the tears started. Lori said, "You aren't alone."

Suddenly I'm relaxed. Completely at peace, feeling blissful, calm, and at one with everything. Then I'm unconscious. I don't recall anything until I realize I'm back in the room lying on my back breathing normally. The music is still going. I open my eyes and see people around me still breathing, wailing, even some up and dancing about. I'm a bit disappointed I didn't go for the whole three hours, but I feel so blissed out it doesn't matter. I look up at Kevin, my sitter who is beside me and tell him, "I think I'm done." Later I learned that two hours had gone by, I thought it was only twenty minutes or so at the time.

One of the professional facilitators, John, comes over and says I still have plenty of time. He suggests I try breathing again and see what happens. I say OK and close my eyes once more.

A few moments into breathing I'm thinking nothing is going to happen because I'm trying too hard, then instantly I'm soaring in some out of body experience and I start laughing at how wrong I was about this being over. Suddenly I'm crying, but with no sad thoughts or emotions behind it. I rock back and forth on the mat to comfort myself. I seem to have no control over my body, but I feel full of love. I keep rocking and it feels great. I feel like I'm in some confined yet comforting place. I want to tell someone I want a hug. I can't speak. I can't move my arms. I cry. I sob and gasp for air lying on my back. I hear the music stop and I know it is time to be over. I slowly open my eyes and look around the room. I feel very out of it, not in my body yet. I cry a bit. I notice Stacia, a facilitator laying by my side on my left. Wow, I wonder how long she's been there, almost spooning

31

me without my knowing. I look to my right at Kevin—he's got the warmest smile I've ever seen. I open my mouth to say something and I start bawling. I'm crying on my back and can't breathe. I sit up to catch my breath. Now that air is flowing, the sobs and tears really come. But again, there is no emotion or thought, just this huge release of...energy I guess. I don't know. I'm on my knees, with my head in my hands on the mat sobbing. Seems like ten minutes of solid bawling. I'm now surrounded by Kevin, John and Stacia. Every time I think it's done I sit up, try to speak, and start crying again. Finally I'm able to spit out that my only thought was that I wanted a hug. I get lots of them.

I still feel like I'm not in my body, especially my arms, they are numb slabs. Kevin and Stacia work with me, holding my arms as I pull against them, to help me get some feeling again. This is my first experience with body work after a breathing session. I stand and feel like I'm walking on the moon. Over the next hour that feeling gradually fades away.

The next phase is drawing a Mandala of the experience, expressing your breathwork on paper. I try to make mine a depiction of all the things I can remember from the experience. My inner nursery schooler thrives, and my drawing looks like it was done by a four year old, but I like it. I write across it, "life is a warm hug."

Mandala #2 Life is a Warm Hug

It wasn't until I was describing my mandala in a small group session that I realized my session seemed to be some sort of prenatal experience and that I was born again. I have felt PHENOMENAL all week. Each workday has even amazed me; everything feels brand new and vibrant. And every hug has been AWESOME.

I'm already signed up for another Holotropic weekend in December. This time my wife, Lori, is joining me. Woohoo!

Looking Back

Looking through my journal a few things I didn't share in my blog post stood out. I had much more tears, energy and movement than my first breathwork two years prior. Yet all the time I was wailing and sobbing my emotions and thoughts felt empty. It was

33

just pure release. I didn't feel sadness, depression or anything after the initial moments of fear when the pressure started. When I told Kevin about my experience and how at one point it felt like my head was on fire he said my head was indeed bright red for a while.

Weeks later I told my mother about my apparent rebirthing and she said the original labor with me was two hours long, the same amount of time as my "contractions" in breathwork. Pretty wild.

The only thing crazier than doing breathwork is watching people do it. While Kevin was rather still and shed a few tears, others in the room seemed flat out possessed doing jaw-dropping yoga moves, crazed dances, some even howled like wolves, while others flailed about on their mat. I sometimes wish I had a video recording of my breathwork to see how strange my tadpole shimmying or dry land breaststroke looked. While I was the sitter for Kevin, I was occasionally overcome with tears and vague emotions I couldn't name. I wrote down, "I love myself and I want to live," which became an affirmation I used for many years to come.

CHAPTER FOUR

The Third Time

JOURNAL ENTRIES - DECEMBER 4-5, 2010

My wife, Lori, joins me for a Holotropic weekend in Pawlet, Vermont where I'm thrilled to see so many people I'd met at my prior breathwork at Kripalu in September. This gathering is a smaller more intimate group of 20 or so people at the home of Lenny and Elizabeth Gibson, certified facilitators who run a sort of Holotropic bed and breakfast.

We were warned against partnering with someone you are in a relationship with, so Lori partners with, Becky, an awesome woman I met at Kripalu. We decide Lori would breathe on Saturday while my breathing session would be Sunday.

For the second consecutive time I partner with Kevin. He breathes on Saturday and we position ourselves near Lori so I can keep an unofficial eye on her too. I was so happy and glad when a few songs into the session, I could see that Lori was having an experience. Kevin had tears a couple songs into his breathwork, but overall less movement and tears than in September.

At times Lori was moving her head, hair and fingers so fast that in the dim light of the room she looked non-human, distorted and animated. It reminded me of the hallucination scenes from the movie "Jacob's Ladder." She seemed to be having a blast as if she was attending a rave on her back. Lori never shed a tear, didn't report any traumatic emotions or memory. She just had fun.

Lori's First Mandala

Lori's experience was so visual she did a second mandala focusing on the geometry she saw. Another participant told her to Google 'sacred geometry' and she discovered the doodling she'd done all her life was this sacred geometry.

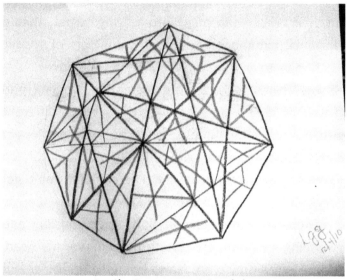

Lori's Geometry Mandala

Following my breathwork on Sunday, this is what I wrote.

Odd. Different. Mystical. Less emotional and more physical than my prior experiences. Lots of extended hand and arm movements. I was playing with energy, controlling it, transforming it, moving it and stretching it like silly putty. Tears of joy rolled down my face at the beauty of holding the Giant Ball of Energy in my hands. It was the Universe.

I could hear other people having a deep experience very quickly and just as I began to think I'd have nothing, I melted into a puddle. At first I was distraught as I dissolved into liquid. Then a Royal Carriage drove over me and I went along for the ride on their tires... I morphed into a flying carpet...then a Universal hammock—becoming some sort of cosmic sail hoping to capture more...energy, good, love.

My hands felt absolutely amazing, tingling and HUGE at times. It was like they were different appendages some times. Hands became giant clam shells grabbing more "good" for me, scooping it up and bringing it towards me. Fears that I can't get "enough."

There were lots of super slow arm extensions and sweeping arcs from my side to up and over my head. At one point they were claws trying to rip things out of me. Other times I was kneading energy like it was dough in my hands.

Then hands raised me up. As if I was dead or being sacrificed on an altar. Then my own hands began to physically rise and play with huge cosmic energy balls.

My hands were gigantic as I rowed and swam across the Universe. I used my giant shell/fan hands to pull goodness and love to me. My arms became wings by the end.

Then it was just pure bliss. Almost a disappointment because "nothing" was going on, but it all felt so cool during it that I can't call it disappointing. Perhaps it was all messages regarding manifesting?

Towards the end of breathwork I was seeing solid things. Some sort of a temple wall built of squares, angles, carved in lines, sort of a Mayan face. Then all sorts of layering of gold letters, but not any alphabet I recognized, appeared and then faded away. It happened too quickly for me to recall details and draw but I really had the sense that it was some sort of language.

I take a seat at the mandala table to draw and almost burst into tears.

In my sharing the following morning I think, "Wow! Was my 'disappointment' in the happy/blissful phase a metaphor? Do I look for the pain in life instead of the bliss? Do I have an expectation of pain not love?

We drove home to Massachusetts that evening and I wrote this in my journal: Whatever happens is the best thing that could happen to me because only the best things happen to me—this is my thought as I drift off to sleep.

A recurring theme continues to be that I'm doing something wrong and am not going to have an experience in my breathwork, yet I always do. And it seems the very moment I think I'm getting nothing this time, the floor falls out from under me and away I go. I really wish I could see what I looked like this time. Kevin said some of my hand and arm movements were beautiful to watch.

Lori ended up across the room and out of direct line of sight of me while I breathed. She said she could hear my sobs and laughs cut through the room at various times and was kind of glad she couldn't see me so she could focus on her partner.

Andy's Mandala #3

Looking Back

This was a breakthrough session for me on many levels. There was no trauma, sadness, pain or constant flow of tears. I broke some of my self-imposed rules and moved my body, experimented and had fun. At times I felt beautiful and artistic in my movements and can still recall marveling at some of my own hand and arm slow-motion contortions. I was beginning to have experiences reminding me of how powerful I was, how much I controlled and what an excellent manifester I am.

It was a great experience to work with Kevin again. We could operate on an almost wordless communication with each other and feel safe to breathe and explore. And I was thrilled that Lori enjoyed it and was hooked to want to do it again. Being close enough to watch her during her session was an honor and provided some amazing sights. She radiated so much joy the entire time, which certainly challenged my views on what breathwork was all about. At the time my own judgments said she was doing it "wrong" since she wasn't crying, but it was great to see that breathwork didn't have to be a heavy, traumatic release. That helped pave the way for my own experiences of joy and bliss.

CHAPTER FIVE

The Fourth Time

BLOG POST - SUNDAY, MARCH 20, 2011

Holotropic Breathwork - March 19, 2011

Yesterday was my fourth Holotropic Breathwork session and Lori's second. It was our first time with the Boston Holotropic group, which made it close and convenient. The best instruction I heard this weekend was, "Breathe until you are surprised."

Yesterday was the first time Lori and I were partners. The first time Lori tried it last December in Vermont we didn't want our relationship/involvement to effect the other person's experience so we paired with other people. Now that we are wily veterans it felt fine to work together, and I'm so glad we did.

This weekend included a group of eight breathers at a time and Lori breathed first. It took roughly ten minutes until I was sure she was having an experience. She had a sleep mask covering her eyes and a blanket pulled up to her chin, so the only thing I could clearly see was her mouth. I've never seen such a beautiful sight. Her smile was almost blinding with joy. She rocked in place to the music and became very verbal and active with her arms. The first words I could make out from her were, "Fly, be free!" She seemed to be throwing things out into the air, and then she was playing with her own hair, tossing it all around having a grand time.

Soon it became clear she was having a full conversation with someone and laughing hysterically throughout it. I knew, and she later confirmed, that she was talking to her dad (who passed away almost 29 years ago). She kept saying such things as, "I know, I know", "I will", "Uh huh", "all right", "ok"... and laughing like a loon much of the time. I had so much fun watching her and feeling the love and joy emanating from that smile. Her laughter filled the room and was infectious. As I made eye contact with other sitters and the facilitators wandering the room, they were all laughing too. I've never seen any breathwork experience like this before. I teased Lori earlier that this is supposed to be traumatic and healing, but she just keeps making it fun. She went overboard this time.

Watching my wife so full of love, life and joy was the most heartwarming experience for me. She's never looked more beautiful to me. A single tear of joy rolled down my face as I lay next to her. I felt like I was witnessing a miracle and I hope that feeling never fades.

At times she sat fully up, laughing like a mad woman, saying "I know, I know", "ok, ok", and "That's silly." She was reminiscing all sorts of stories and memories with her dad. Once I heard her say "That's f'd up", because she couldn't swear in front of her dad. She seemed to be having the time of her life and it was an honor to be in her presence. This lasted for over an hour then it slowly faded away and she got quiet and still with occasional bursts of physical movement. After about two hours and fifteen minutes she opened her eyes and was ready to stop.

Here is Lori's mandala.

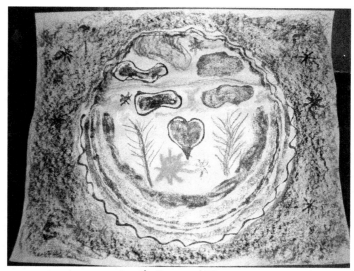

Lori's Second Time

My breathing session was in the afternoon and this one was unlike any other. My prior three experiences had a lot of tears, sobs and pain. This time... it seemed just like a really deep meditation. I felt very protected, blessed and that things were healing, yet there were very little visuals, I barely budged the entire time and I didn't have any vivid memories or experiences. At some points I wondered if I'd fallen asleep even. Then suddenly the music stopped and I thought, this can't be over—no more than an hour could have passed yet. When I opened my eyes, there were no other breathers in the room, Lori was sitting by my side, and it was three hours later. She thought I went very deep and had quite an experience because I moved so little and she said there were multiple times it seemed I'd stopped breathing completely. Friday night the workshop leader mentioned something called "blue-lip bliss", a meditative state so deep that some people forget to breathe. That seemed to be where I ended up. I was very aware of the people, sounds and movement around me. I could tell others were having quite vivid experiences, people were screaming crying, pounding the floor... I did my best not to feel disappointed and just let whatever happens happen. I had a few visuals, like I was in some universe sized snow globe, protected and safe. The last thing I recall seeing was a gold crown, which made me laugh as it reminded me of Monty Python and the Holy Grail. It was like I was seeing my quest or something.

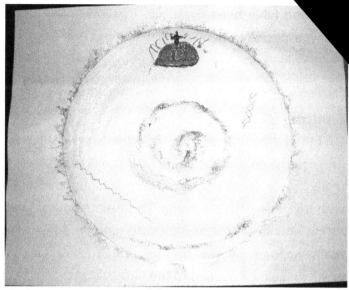

Andy's Mandala

Anyway, I got up from my mat quite easily and went to draw my mandala, which was rather bland as I "saw" so little this time. The mandala is a little arts and crafts project you do after your breathing session. Before you even speak about what happened to anyone you put it on paper. It is another way to integrate your experience.

In the closing session someone said, "I've done a lot of drugs in my life, but nothing gets me high like this does." I couldn't agree more. If you like new experiences or are into personal exploration, you owe it to yourself to try Holotropic Breathwork.

Much more went on in my breathing session that I'm aware of because I slept for over 11 hours last

47

overcome by tears a few times
 I recall watching Lori.

Looking Back

I think this session is my favorite. Not so much for my experience, but for being able to witness Lori's. It really was a stunning, spiritual connection she made with her father that morning. This breathwork proved to me how powerful being a sitter can be. Magic can really happen via the breath. It is such a blessed privilege being a witness to the miraculous.

Three years later, I again breathed with the same group of facilitators who were at this session and they were still talking about the time Lori's session filled the room with an infectious joy and laughter.

CHAPTER SIX

The Fifth Time

BLOG POST - MONDAY, SEPTEMBER 19, 2011

Totally Awesome To Be Alive!

Saturday was my fifth experience with Holotropic Breathwork and the second time Lori and I teamed up as partners. This was a weekend event held at Kripalu in Western Massachusetts and featured the now annual visit from the creator of Holotropic Breathwork, Dr. Stan Grof. It had only been about six months since our prior breathwork, but I really wanted Lori to have the experience of hearing lectures and stories directly from Stan. Since he is in his eighties, I'm not sure how many more opportunities we might have to hear him.

49

Once again it was unlike any prior time. I fell into a very deep meditative state even before the music and breathing was supposed to start. Suddenly I found myself lying on my mat, realizing the tribal music was cranking and I needed to get breathing fast. I had no idea how much time had passed and I thought "Oh no! I'm missing it."

This went on a few times; I thought I wasn't getting much out of it. I had very few conscious memories or experiences. I was either in the room thinking I was missing it or I was in some zone so deep I got no "story" from it. I remember laughing out loud a few times at my thoughts that I wasn't getting anything - some part of me knew better. A few times when the bass of the music had the floor vibrating it felt like every cell of mine was vibrating and ascending. As I floated above into some golden dimension, I took one step forward and completely lost my balance and "landed" back on the mat, in the room, with the music cranking and people breathing and wailing around me. I laughed again. I felt like someone was saying, "Ah, you think you are ready for this enlightenment? Think again kid!" I was considering opening my eyes with a disappointed feeling when the music stopped. Three hours had gone by—wow.

Yesterday I felt out of it, wondering what I was integrating since I didn't have much memory of things

happening in my breathwork session. But today I woke up feeling so ALIVE, so AWESOME that I declared it to be Totally Awesome to Be Alive Day.
Totally Awesome to Be Alive Day Video
http://youtu.be/tA41oeHrbdw

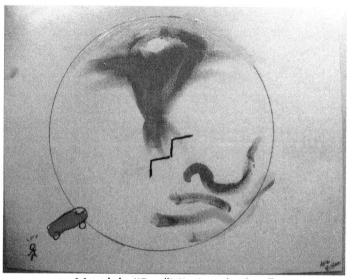

Mandala #5 – "Missing the bus"

Lori enjoyed her experience and looked gorgeous as she went on her ride. She was doing all sorts of cool motions with her hands, sort of a mix of sculpting and dancing at times. She sat up on a number of occasions and it took all my control not to wrap her up in a hug.

Her session ended in a very cool way as the creator of this process and a founding father of Transpersonal Psychology, 80-year-old Stan Grof lay

51

down next to her and held her hand. She opened her eyes and looked at him like a new-born baby. She said, "The Universe is purple! Do you see it?" Stan, replied "No, but I'm glad you do." She added, "No matter how much you give, it all comes back to you."

It was beautiful to watch. Ever since that weekend she often dies a bit of her hair purple.

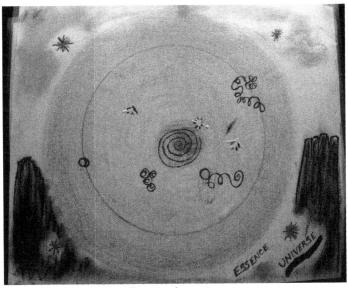

Lori's purple universe

Looking Back

Even today in April of 2014, I have to laugh when looking back at this session because Lori still dies some of her hair purple. In fact, last week she died all of her hair a bright, vibrant purple. It also delights me that she got some personal time with Stan Grof, even though at first she thought it was me who had touched her and she was bit pissed off that I'd interrupted her experience.

For me, it took a while to accept that a nice, calm, pleasant session was ok. I had to let go of my previous experiences and trust that I got exactly what I needed. I had to have faith that healing and growth are occurring and that I hadn't missed anything.

CHAPTER SEVEN

The Sixth Time

BLOG POST - SUNDAY, MARCH 11, 2012

The Joyous Millipede

Yesterday I took part in my sixth Holotropic experience and it was the most fun-filled one yet. My prior experiences have ranged from traumatic roller coaster rides of emotion, with lots and lots of tears, to extremely blissful meditations free of any visuals or sensations.

In fact, my prior session in September 2011 was so uneventful I was in no rush to breathe again. Luckily, I've turned Lori onto this and she wanted to do it again. This weekend was her fourth time and the third time we were partners.

Lori breathed first and seemed to have a very happy and content experience. Her hands flowed and danced about while she had a big beaming smile on her face for almost the entire first hour. Then she went into a long period of stillness and quiet only to have a more visible experience singing and sliding about on her mat for another twenty minutes before being quiet and still again until the music stopped after 2 1/2 hours.

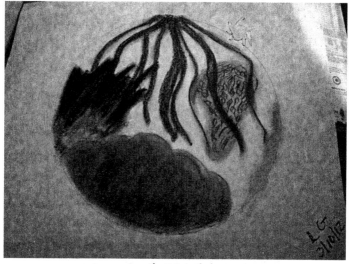

Lori's Mandala

This round for me was the first time I truly had no expectations. I had already had life changing experiences and other sessions that felt like glorified naps, whatever was going to show up today—I was cool with it. I was rewarded with a very cool and joyous ride. It was the most flat out fun I've ever had in breathwork. There wasn't a single tear shed.

55

The music is such a huge component of breathwork and the soundtrack was full of great tribal drumming and the most vocalization I'd encountered. None of it was in English, but I was converting some of it into messages that fueled my experience.

I don't really recall the music starting. There was a point I felt like I'd just landed on the mat, noticed the music was cranking and I thought I better get my breath cranking because I have no idea how long I've zoned out for. I started my deep, non-stop breathing and the music had all sorts of singing in some language, I'll guess Hindi, which started creating the most amazing scene. It was a combination of Muppet sort of folks, dozens of Plush Larry The Lizard's, and the Star Wars cantina band. Characters were all sorts of shapes and sizes, a few blue puffy guys were even playing the cello. I was smiling so much, filled with such joy and entertainment I was laughing out loud as I lay on the mat with my eyes closed. This "show" went on for a while and it felt like the most fun I could ever have inside my head—or where ever this was happening. At times all the Plush Larry's created a chorus and were singing to the music playing in the room.

At one point I realized I was a millipede and I was racing through the jungle trying to get to the source of the music before the song stopped. It was a very tribal sounding piece of music with some singing and I wanted to find the people and join in on the fun. On the mat I was moving my feet, legs and shoulders a lot - in fact Lori later told me I was moving my mat and lots of the stuff around me, but my arms weren't used. Which makes perfect sense since I was a millipede. As the tempo of the music sped up I moved faster and faster, yet my millipede self never felt panicked. He was so digging the music, full of joy, he/I just hoped to find the party before they stopped. At one point I burst out laughing again because I saw an old blue VW bus and Hurley from "Lost" was driving. He yelled out an encouraging, "Dude!" to me and was gone.

The music changed to another track but it was close enough in theme to keep my millipede-self going and I came upon a fire where a bunch of natives were dancing and celebrating. I tried to stand up and join in. I wanted to dance with them. But millipedes can't stand up. I kept trying and falling down. But there was no sense of frustration. There was never a time when I was going to give up. Trying was fun. It made me think about learning to walk - that kids just keep trying and the trying is fun. During the time I'm shifting, squirming and shimmying up and down my mat and I was going into a bridge pose trying to get my millipede-self standing up. It was an insane amount of fun.

Next thing I recall was that my legs turned to roots and I became one with the earth. I started having a bit of ayahuasca flashbacks and swear that old taste was in my mouth as I became a plant and then the earth. So I was the entire planet for a while, knowing, realizing and feeling that all the creatures and people I had seen were me. They were part of me and created by me all at the same time. Then some metamorphosis happened I shot up into the sky as pure energy and spent something between 20 minutes and a millennia soaring through the cosmos and floating amongst the stars.

Pretty, pretty cool.

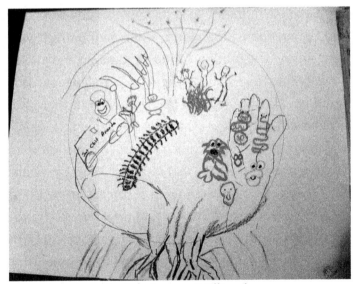

Andy's Joyous Millipede

Looking Back

It is a rather bizarre feeling for me to have so much fun in breathwork. My first few Holotropic experiences were such traumatic, emotional releases that truly changed the direction of my life; I almost feel that I've done something wrong when I just have fun, but "just having fun" was all I wanted in my most depressed times. My own views on breathwork were slowly changing and I was allowing myself to grow from fun as well as from tears. I no longer see these joy-filled experiences as something I've done "wrong" or that I missed out on some deep-seated release. Yet, I wouldn't feel drawn to another breathwork session for two years.

CHAPTER EIGHT

The Seventh Time

BLOG POST - SUNDAY, FEBRUARY 2, 2014

World Dance Party

Yesterday I took part in my seventh Holotropic Breathwork and it was by far the most celebratory one I've done. From the very first moments I was laughing and dancing on my mat, having a grand ol' time.

For those who don't know; Holotropic Breathwork is a group event of self-exploration that uses rapid, deep breathing and loud, evocative music (think tribal drumming, instrumentals, ancient chants, nothing has English lyrics) to enter a non-ordinary state of consciousness. It can seem very much like an acid trip, but you aren't under the influence of anything except for yourself. After breathwork you draw your experience in a mandala. I can't draw for shit (especially after a 2 1/2 hour Holotropic trip), but I love my mandalas. I even wrote a book about my prior Holotropic Breathwork experiences because I want more people to know about this process and give it a try.

My session was very music driven. At the start I was tiny and jumping on guitar and piano strings trying to avoid the one being struck, then as the music became more drumming tracks I was hiding under different drum heads, avoiding being struck. It was all a fun game. I felt like I was part of a con man's shell game, that I was the pea. Even though I'm actually just lying on my back on a matt and this is all happening in my mind (or in some other realm?) I was dancing, swaying, and gyrating to the music the whole time.

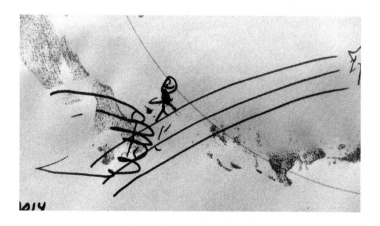

Dancing On Guitar Strings

As the songs went on, I found myself in this huge underground dance club all carved out of stone. It looked like Stonehenge had been rebuilt as some sort of Goth, gay, fetish, dance club. I was like a tourist being shown all around and these huge German muscle men that were dripping in sweat and oil kept coming up to me saying, "We want to oil you up." I laughed out loud each time, because they kept reminding me of the Saturday Night Live characters, Hanz and Franz, saying "We want to pump you up!"

Orgies

There was a different style of mayhem and debauchery in every corner of this place; it had orgies, hula dancers, African Masai warrior dancers, people pouring hot wax onto each other, and all sorts of scenes out of something like "Eyes Wide Shut." It seemed like every culture and every fetish was represented and I just kept laughing at each new sight, each new discovery. The music was cranking, the bass was pumping, lights and glitter were flying everywhere—then the Pope arrived! He was atop the whole scene in an elevated DJ booth. Turns out this secret underground club is beneath the Vatican!

The Pope's Underground Club

The Pope was going totally sick throwing streamers and glitter all around, loving everyone, reigning over the debauchery and fun. The Germans kept offering to oil me up and tried teaching my different dances. I just laughed and laughed and laughed. Everyone was insanely buff and gorgeous (like when Homer Simpson tells a story and he looks like Hercules in his mind.) I said to people around me that this was some sort of demented Dance Party USA, the Pope yelled out, "No! It's Dance Party Universe!"

The music slowed down a bit and became this amazing, heavy bass riff. I turned to follow a couple German muslceheads into a tunnel. Actually we were all earthworms now and were creating a tunnel through the rock and dirt to leave the Pope's bash. We burrowed and tunneled further and further into the ground, as the bass kept getting louder and deeper, shaking everything around us.

We finally broke through to some sort of cave and there was Nikki Sixx from Motley Crüe, Gene Simmons from Kiss and the Devil all playing bass. Nothing but bass, and it ROCKED! We were all headbanging in hell! The Devil had this amazing red, glass upright bass. He said he was just a misunderstood character out for some fun. It was all I could do to not leap up on my mat and start throwing my fists in the air. It was like I was at the best, most intense concert ever. It was definitely turned up to 11!

Hell Bass Jam

The music moved into a slower, lighter, orchestral section and I ascended up out of hell. It was still very much in a rock and roll theme as I was raised up on some infinite rising platform straight out of a KISS stage show. As I rose higher and higher, I received messages of, you are much more than that, and you have a bigger role than to just rock out. This was the first period of tears in my breathwork. (Unlike my initial breathwork experiences a few years ago which were nothing but tears.) I was overwhelmed with love and joy, also with a sense of purpose and meaning. I was shedding tears of joy, not pain or sadness. I was told I'm a "Lighter of Light" - which is a phrase I've heard repeatedly in recent months as I've worked in my Akashic Record.

Lighter of Light

Then I entered a very serene and peaceful period; similar to a very deep state of meditation. It was timeless and blissful. I recall one scene of yelling at my wife, Lori, who wasn't there, "Enough with the raisins!" Every time she comes across food with raisins in it she goes on and on about how much she hates raisins, and raisins ruin food. Muffins and cookies with raisins were served that day and that all popped into my mind somewhere between Heaven and hell.

The only other time I remember crying was when I felt my late dog Homer's presence. Homer is actually part of a book by Louise Hay and David Kessler coming out on February 4, 2014, called "You Can Heal Your Heart". Sobbing, I asked Homer if he was happy with what I've done with his lessons, his story. He was. He told me he was proud of me and so appreciated my work in spreading his wisdom. The book from Louise Hay comes out exactly 1 year and 1 month from the day Homer was killed. Then I saw our first cat, Garfield. I remember saying, "You guys didn't even know each other." Many years passed between Garfield getting killed by coyotes and us getting Homer. They said, we know each other now! And then our other deceased cat, Samantha, whom did share our home with Homer also sauntered by. The music transitioned into a beautiful harp composition and Homer was now playing the harp with his tail.

Homer The Harp Playing Hound

I was filled with so much love, peace and joy. I wallowed in those emotions for the remainder of my time. When I opened my eyes about 2 1/2 hours after I'd closed them, I didn't feel out of it or disoriented. I was so ready to get to my mandala; I had been drawing it in my mind all along. Wishing I had the skill the get the amazing scenes in my head onto paper. But alas, I'm still a kindergartener when it comes to marking up paper.

Here is the entire mandala.

Dance Party Universe!

At home that night, Lori and I were watching *Saturday Night Live* and one of my favorite characters, Stefon, showed up again. Stefon is the city correspondent on Weekend Update and I realized that my Dance Party Universe was one of Stefon's insanely described clubs. "This place has everything..." If you aren't familiar with Stefon, just search YouTube for "Stefon SNL".

Looking Back

Beyond being such an outlandish, fantastic, even ecstatic time that had me in a great mood for many days, this breathwork was special because I introduced a friend to Holotropic Breathwork. At the start of the day she was nervous and scared, asking, "Why would anyone do this more than once?"

Three hours later, it was "I can't wait to do this again!"

Now that I've had two consecutive breathwork sessions of pure joy and fun, I wonder if I've released all the emotional pain and trauma I need to – at least for now. I went almost two full years between my last two sessions because I thought this had to be a big emotional ordeal, but I no longer feel that way. Seeing my friend have such a wonderful first experience, and seeing my wife have multiple very enjoyable experiences over the years have finally got me to the point where I'm allowing myself to simply enjoy the ride. Here's to many more great rides!

CHAPTER NINE

Closing

I hope this glimpse into my experiences with Holotropic Breathwork has intrigued you enough to explore it for yourself. I still get emotional reading some of my own accounts. The options for breathwork programs range from single-day, to weekend-long and full-week programs too. I certainly plan to do breathwork again, and fully expect it to be a tool I use for the rest of my life.

I recently got to spend some time with Kevin, my two-time sitter, for the first time in a couple years and our rapport was like we see each other all the time. In fact, I'm still in touch with many people I've met at Holotropic Breathwork events. That is the power of your breath.

I share breathwork as a powerful modality whenever I speak about my experiences with depression and suicidal thinking. I hope to turn more people on to Holotropic Breathwork and look forward to sharing many more of my adventures. People I've met who've done this many dozens of times say no two are the same and it never gets old.

I've finally let myself be at the point where I can look forward to it as simply a wonderfully, joyous and spiritual experience. I no longer carry requirements of trauma and tears into my breathwork sessions. Some of my happiest and most life-affirming times have been in Holotropic Breathwork. That has proven to me that I'm worthy of and can create similar times in my "normal" life too.

About The Author

My name is Andy Grant. I am a husband, writer, actor, speaker, transformational energy coach, photographer, children's book author, filmmaker, workshop leader, world traveler and lifelong learner. I've also spent years battling depression and suicidal thoughts. In fact, I've made multiple attempts on my own life.

Holotropic Breathwork is the most healing practice I've ever come across. It has helped me tremendously and I hope it serves you too.

Learn more about me at www.NavitasCoach.com

Resources

The creators of Holotropic Breathwork, Stanislav Grof
and Christina Grof, have written many books. These
are just a few of them.

*Holotropic Breathwork: A New Approach to Self-
Exploration and Therapy* by Stanislav Grof and
Christina Grof
Stanislav Grof and Christina Grof describe their
groundbreaking new form of self-exploration and
psychotherapy: Holotropic Breathwork. The
breathwork utilizes the remarkable healing and
transformative potential of non-ordinary states of
consciousness. These states engender a rich array of
experiences with unique healing potential--reliving
childhood memories, infancy, birth and prenatal life,
and elements from the historical and archetypal
realms of the collective unconscious.

When the Impossible Happens: Adventures in Non-Ordinary Reality by Stanislav Grof
Feelings of oneness with other people, nature, and the universe. Encounters with extraterrestrials, deities, and demons. Out-of-body experiences and past-life memories. Science casts a skeptical eye. But Dr. Stanislav Grof—the psychiatric researcher who cofounded transpersonal psychology—believes otherwise.

The Stormy Search for the Self: A Guide to Personal Growth through Transformational Crisis by Stanislav Grof and Christina Grof
Christina and Stanislav Grof, the world's foremost authorities on the subject of spiritual emergence, draw on years of dramatic personal and professional experience with transformative states to explore these "spiritual emergencies," altered states so powerful they threaten to overwhelm the individual's ordinary reality.

Psychology of the Future: Lessons from Modern Consciousness Research by Stanislav Grof
This accessible and comprehensive overview of the work of Stanislav Grof, one of the founders of transpersonal psychology, was specifically written to acquaint newcomers with his work. Serving as a summation of his career and previous works, this book is the source to introduce Grof's enormous

contributions to the fields of psychiatry and psychology, especially his central concept of holotropic experience, where holotropic signifies "moving toward wholeness."

Websites

ABHI
www.abhi.org
The Association for Holotropic Breathwork International (AHBI) is a worldwide non-profit, membership-operated organization of Holotropic Breathwork facilitators, participants, academics and therapists. The AHBI website is a major resource for anyone interested in Holotropic Breathwork.

Grof Transpersonal Training
www.holotropic.com
The main site for Holotropic Breathwork information and training.

StanislavGrof.com
www.stanislavgrof.com
Stan's site listing his many books, appearances and events.

Boston Holotropic
bostonholotropic.com
Boston Holotropic is a dedicated group of experienced

Grof-certified Holotropic Breathwork™ facilitators, facilitators of other modalities, trainees and supporting participants.

Vermont Holotropic
www.dreamshadow.com
Elizabeth and Lenny are Grof–certified Holotropic Breathwork facilitators. They have raised their two sons on a hillside at their homestead in Pawlet, Vermont, where they have built a retreat center and offered workshops since 1994.

Kripalu Center for Yoga and Health
www.kripalu.org
A world renowned spiritual center in the Berkshires of Western Massachusetts. Kripalu is a nonprofit educational organization dedicated to empowering people and communities to realize their full potential through the transformative wisdom and practice of yoga.

Holosync by Centerpointe Meditate like a Zen monk at the touch of a button Holosync is a CD system that I use for my meditation practice. You can get a free demo at www.centerpointe.com/?aid=369941 and try it yourself.

Andy's Other Books

200 Positive Powerful Affirmations and 6 Simple Tips to Put Them to Work (For You!)
An Amazon best-seller, 200 Powerful Positive Affirmations and 6 Simple Tips to Put Them To Work, contains more than 200 uplifting affirmations to replace the automatic negative thoughts most people's days are full of. This collection includes author Andy Grant's personal favorites--the ones that helped him overcome years of pessimistic thinking, depression, and suicidal thoughts. The affirmations are broken down into six categories for easy reference.

AffirmVol2 200 Powerful Positive Affirmations Volume II and 6 Super Chargers to Put Them To Work
More valuable than the affirmations are the explorations into why affirmations work for some but not others. In 200 Powerful Positive Affirmations Volume II and 6 Super Chargers to Put Them To Work, Andy Grant shares an additional 200 (actually many more) uplifting affirmations to replace the automatic negative thoughts most people's days are full of. You will dig deep into resistance, and learn six new super chargers to get the most out of your work with positive affirmations and to create your own. Also

included is a link to free audios and videos to make the book serve you even more.

Homer the Hound Dog's Guide to Happiness: 6 Life Lessons I Learned From My Dog!

When author, Andy Grant's, dog Homer (affectionately called Homey) died suddenly in early January, 2013 it was one of the most emotionally painful events in his life. Homer had been by his side every day for over nine years. In his initial days of grief Andy began to realize all the wonderful things Homer taught him. He even consulted an animal communicator, or pet psychic. The messages received from Homer confirmed that Andy had to write this book. This is the full story of the Homer featured in Louise Hay's *You Can Heal Your Heart.*

The Globetrotting Adventures of Larry The Lizard: Larry In the Amazon

Larry in The Amazon is a children's photo book for ages 4-8. It features actual photographs of Larry The Lizard's adventure in the Amazon rainforest of Peru. Larry's story includes meeting piranhas, monkeys, a tapir, the Yagua Indians, and much more. Larry The Lizard is a plastic lizard who believes in living life to the fullest. Larry loves to explore new places, meet new people, and learn new things, from his own backyard to the wonders of the world.

Lightning Source UK Ltd.
Milton Keynes UK
UKOW05f2326171016

285528UK00018B/472/P